# Women of Words

# Women of Words
## 2016 – 2018

Edited by Janette Hoppe

Papatuanuku Press

First published in 2020
Published by Papatuanuku Press
260 Christo Road
Waratah NSW 2298

hoponin@bigpond.net.au

NATIONAL
LIBRARY
OF AUSTRALIA

A catalogue record for this book is available from the National Library of Australia

ISBN      9780992478230

Cover design by David Musgrave

Cover art image © Rhiannon Pryor

Printed by Lightning Source International

# Contents

# Acknowledgements

The Women of Words Project would not have been as successful if it was not for the generosity of the Newcastle community and the wonderful women and men who have supported this project.

I'd like to thank all the poets who have contributed their art, time and voices to this project. Especially those who have been involved from the beginning with the original chapbook and events throughout November 2016. The women who are included in this book have featured as part of the project 2016-2018.

I'd like to thank the venues that have supported and continue to support this project: Vinyl Café, The Press Book House, Good Brothers Espresso and Hudson Street Hum.

I'd like to thank Debbie Robson (Starving in a Garrett) for supporting this project and co-hosting the Women of Words events 2016-2017. I'd like to thank Gillian Swain for co-hosting the Women of Words events 2018-2019.

I'd like to thank Rhiannon Pryor for the cover art of this new publication of Women of Words. I'd like to thank the artists from *Women of Words – Eat, Stray'd, Love:* Pernille Oldham for the cover art; Cecilia White for the images accompanying the poet's biographies; and Rhiannon Pryor for providing her own self portrait image. Thank you to the artists that have contributed artworks for the silent auctions: Arohanoa Mathews, Deborah Thacker McDonald and Belinda Street.

I'd like to thank Anna Forsyth from Girls on Key for her editing expertise and collating of this current Women of Words publication. I'd like to thank Catherine Knight for the final editorial counsel. Finally, thank you Ed Wright, David Musgrave and the team at Puncher and Wattmann for publishing this phenomenal book of words.

Mauri Ora,
Janette Hoppe
(Papatuanuku Press)

# Foreword

The Women of Words Project was created in 2016 as a response to the alarming death toll of women and children by the hands of their loved ones. The initial project sought submissions from women to share their voices and shine the light on Domestic and Family Violence through a collaborative chapbook of poetry. In 2016 Papatuanuku Press published *Women of Words – Eat, Stray'd, Love*.

The book launch was organised for November 2016 at a local café in Newcastle with readings from contributors. During this planning stage, acclaimed poet Judy Johnson asked how she could contribute if Domestic and Family Violence wasn't her story. A plan was set into action to see if there were other women that would like to be involved and a subsequent event held the following day to celebrate women was organised. Due to the overwhelming response from the poetry community another three events were organised raising funds for Hunter Women's Centre and White Ribbon Australia.

In 2017 the Women of Words Project claimed the last Sunday in November to host the Women of Words event to raise funds for local charities that support women and children escaping domestic violence. This has become an annual tradition featuring a phenomenal line-up of female poets and spoken word artists.

In 2018 Women of Words Project was included in the Newcastle Writer's Festival and will continue to evolve much like the nature of Women and Words.

# Maireener shells at the Painted Cliffs, Maria Island

*Dael Allison*

The naming is gone, the syntax of colours,
their meaning, who made them.
I knot green weed in your hair, you paint
mine with ochre, touch each pale breast.
This is long-leg women's place
the low sun tells me. When men come here
they know it and gullet their words.

The cunted cliffs suck salt and time,
young girls point and giggle —
in the litany of lines and stains
they understand what men do,
and birth.

Here old women collected slow handfuls
of shells, rubbed them with ash,
sought the nacreous
creation spiral, its green beginning —
their language for this
unsayable now. Try it
your mouth will purse
like a dry womb. Spit sand.

We search for shells to string
against obscurity, to unweave
the dark ghosts. We call back
the knowing ones,
their fathomless eyes.

# Welcome to Fear City

*Magdalena Ball*

this is the city but it's not a city
it's embodied mind

everyone walks because it's too hot
air conditioning is broken
garbage rots on the street
spilling into the parking spots

the city is in debt for three million
and no pre-nuptial

black plastic bags mount the sidewalks
with no traffic cops on duty
everyone angry
the parallel fracture

moving outward from the heart
to the cracks in the sidewalk
the embodied city couldn't pay
its workers went on strike

bags were splitting and I got mugged
hard butt of a gun against my back
embodied as garbage, a toy, a throwaway
salvaged from the rubbish bags
pressing into pale skin

the city was a river but it flooded
water mixed with leaked gas
on the darkening street the trains were late
doors wouldn't open

city went broke
concrete cracking into liquid fissures
in the gutter down side streets

the strike ended just before Christmas
70,000 tonnes of trash were cleaned
including the unwanted detritus of another
failed marriage
left to memory in front of an
abandoned apartment building
like a forgotten promise.

# Dreams in Life

*Lisa Barron*

Dreams do not die.
We just forget them
Life deals its lot.
We fit into our slot.
Dreams now covered
With the grime of our life.
We just get on with it,
Want no strife,
Stick to a routine.
Keep your house clean
Take care with where you are seen
And never daydream.
Work hard
Take it easy
Nothing ceases,

Numbed to the bone,
Successful though.
Living in a beautiful home.
Alone in stone
Chaos strikes.
We question our life.
Plans are shattered, as though nothing mattered.
We writhe in the pain of losing a game.

We lay naked, exposed.
Our heart fully closed; nothing is clear.
Until in the silence of an empty heart,
We hear our spirit whisper,
Things are not as they seem.

It's simply the resurgence of your dream.
Stop the chatter of your head,
And look with an open heart instead.
Cleared of your old shackles
You are free to make a start.
Let your heart lead and not your head
You'll see your dream is waiting up ahead.

# Double Standards

*Louise Berry*

many say women of thirty or more
are lost without a partner
without a child
to care for them as they age

yet

don't criticize those men
who study hard
work hard
have no spare time

put

a career ahead of relationships
never learn to get along
with others
believe only in themselves

scorn

breeders
those who provide
the next generation
to buy their services

yet

have one-night stands
reject the results
blame women
for trapping them

are


as caring as a
Bengal tiger
intent on prey
satisfying basic urges

enough

# Duty of care

*Kelly Blaney-Murphy*

She stayed out
beyond the breakers
as long as she dared
making sure to come in
while she still had strength.
(Once she had not and
the shore lay out of reach.
Finally, he'd swum out to help).

Face-down on her towel, hiding
the way her tired breasts
made one lumpy mound
in last year's swimmers,
her mind unravelled in poetry
where not completely caught
comparing sensation –
sea-breeze-pimpled legs
versus sun-groggy shoulders.
Stretched by the first swim of spring,
consistent wash of waves
onto beach lulled her:
the world went on.
Until, in the sand beside her,
eyes closed behind glasses,
he said, I haven't seen
our children for a while.

Then she had to think of them,
those two beauties on the cusp
of all of this, lured into the black

hummocks behind the No Camping sign
by boys who didn't mind breaking rules,
or flailing unheard as mangrove mud
sucked them in, or tossed
like discarded party favours
on the rocks the other end of the bay.

# Rebirth Rising

*Lisa Callister*

Feet on the earth
Roots pushing down,
As nobody's anything
Stood solid on the ground.
Body tall and strong
Arms branching out wide
That sunward tilt, breathing in
Acknowledging the day, received as given.
The twists, the bends, the knowing, the quirks
All imperfectly perfect at one with the dirt
Evergreen yet shedding
Renewing, emerging, fresh life beginning
At one with the universe
The seed began living.

# White Ribbon

*Jan Dean*

Picture a stunning bride in white
covered in blood.  Days of suffering
come to an end, in violence.
When I thought about dresses
for the dead, my tangent took me
faraway from fact.  A group made
sixty-eight dresses, one for every woman
in our country murdered by her partner
so far this year.  I won't mess
around with metaphors.  It's enough
to think they died at the hands of someone
once loved and admired.

What do angels wear?  Gossamer
trails, pale as air, or suits of silver
to bulletproof the bare.  There's
a narrow ribbon of white, connecting
angels to new clothes back there.

# Birthday

*Gloria Demillo*

How her hips snapped for you, the deep crimson
Spilling between legs,
She is the serpent who devours herself, ouroboros.
Gives you her mouth, the roadwork of her feet
When you cry it is an echo, a sad nursery rhyme
Dipped in your mother's tongue.

Once she pulls the feeble thing from insider her,
She gives you a name which means you are a miracle,
A blessing twenty-four days too early; this birth is easily a mourning.
Buries placenta near grandfather's ashen body;
Tradition which ties you to earth.
As she wraps you in the neighbour's clothes;
Something new, something borrowed,
Is how you begin to think of time
As you drift within the rooms
Of your mother's cavernous life.
When you say her name, Estrellita
It becomes an echo
Inday, anak…

# Sydney

*Meg Dunn*

you loud and raucous harbour bastard
you pump and seethe
and the mercury ain't dipped from 31 since this summer started raining
big fat drops and a real estate boom,
your sexy frangipani giggling green
with the last chance of a rainbow
in that shaft of last sunlight on the Bridge you'd sell to China.

You pump and heave like your ferries, brutish tugboats,
your thuggish local members,
council developers, unattended football fests, police with a sniffer,
from North Rocks to Bennelong to the Cross up to Chatswood, out to
                                                    Baulkham Hills
you're bent on the take and taking the piss
making a fuss about nothing much,
cicada songs strafing your crumbling terraces, seen to be in the way
                                                    of progress.

Sydney
you are dreadlocked palm trees in singlets and thongs, a razor cut
dripping convict attitudes like dropped cricket catches in a
                                                    pocket park,
it looks like you are skating fast but relaxation is shoplifting and
                                                    damage music,
traditional over-drinking,
swanning around with your belly protruding and your gut muscles
                                                    clenched
throwing love pats at the missus in the barbeque hours,
coppers hold protestors face down so you can bulldoze parks and
                                                    build exclusive towers.

Your bullish masculinity swings dicks or fists and then frocks up in
pride
confused, you buy the wife a talking car, yet kiss the handbag dog,
fruit bats are common and noxious, Hillsong is yet to sight God,
unconcerned gays stroke their catalogues, layer lasagne,
cockroaches flock like junk mail, your morals are a tangle of lantana.
Your trains are filthy and the Gap to mind is something to be
jumped off
lattes curdle in 36 degrees, no wonder your overwhelming
attitude is anxious.


Sydney
your drive-time DJs butt-lick traffic ears to the static jam
as red tail lights make FM songlines through the dark
from IKEA to Belleview Hill, Bunnings to Bardwell Park.
Front-bar would-be jailbirds play pool spraying too much pesticide,
a lone nurse after midnight is taken for a last ride from a lonely
station
jasmine climbs the paling fences
weaving night-air perfume through your jangled, misplaced senses
as a crime takes place.


Your Rum Corps ethics are rife and firing,
rain drops heavy sentences from silks in courts all thunder
while rampant paedophilia gets the judges retiring,
violent bougainvillea blooms with thorns on property lines
Maseraties at Bondi, kebabs in Marrickville at dawn
the mercury is rising as mosquitos swarm,
your headlines are inclined to scream the nightmares from the great
Australian dream.

Sydney
your west gapes in horrid neglect
pollies stamp on the pedal of deals to run over the housing
commission,
ICAC swats at another corrupt decision to mine your last
farming acre
as the long arm of the law gets iced over in the fibro streets of
Blacktown
brick throwing at the bowlo, lights out at the RSL,
lest we forget, Sydney, you're a piss taker!
The rest of the state is scaling your detritus, watching your
actions, wary of your hubris.

Your Domain soapbox has no tongue
Eora Nation barely speaks, barani is a vacant cry for yesterday
when Bennelong lay down and died and no-one buying
remembers why.
Your bat-cape Aussie flags are wrapped around your last two
tinnies dragging in the dirt and piss
of happy whiteman dominance,
and your land is girt by backroom deals for shiny casinos and a
price beyond all sense —
the rest of us are watching and waiting for the reckoning of
your hubris and your recompense.

Apologies to anyone who is 'from' Sydney. To anyone who has been 'of'
Sydney or who knows of Sydney and its first -foot dominance and rum
corps ethos over the whole country's colonisation, it's not to be helped, but
it can be questioned.

# Your brain on poetry

*Anna Forsyth*

I see it, prismatic
your words refract and split
in glorious ways
curious ways
kaleidoscopic delight.

Your words are evidence
of your bird's-eye view
of the way light plays
in elusive twists and turns.

Your beautiful
poem brain flees logic
swoops to catch meaning
lets it loose
and we gasp.

Your brain
that beautiful poem machine
defies logic
I imagine it lighting up
channelling words
to surprise.

I see it there
inside your skull, a prism
your words refract
shapes of language
forming new delights.

Most hold only grey matter
within their skulls
when you speak
you re-write light
logic shuts its mouth
and even language is shocked
it feels itself
refracted
in glorious ways
broken open
to its own hidden
stain glass messages.

Did you know you are Picasso
of light and sound
or is speaking in multiple
dimensions, child's play?

Where some house grey matter
ghoulish red, bulging brains
inside your poet skull
I know there is
an indescribable prism.

Maybe one day
they'll scan your brain
an exercise in understanding
how light is born
in multiple directions
they'll open it up
but find the prism of it
unreadable
except by heart.

When you write
you swoop above
language itself
as if exempt from gravity
we are taken up
captured
we are hawk and hare
both.

You are a maestro of refraction
your words reflect
the shock
of multiplicity
so often misconstrued
but I swoop
with you, warp speed
both hawk and hare
that beautiful prism
channelling rainbows
and we gasp
we gasp.

# Anatomy

*Debra Hely*

Once upon a time
in another life
I used to teach
I enjoyed teaching
one of my biggest challenges
in human reproduction
was finding good illustrations
it took me years
but finally, there it was
a textbook picture
with labels clearly pointing
naming, validating, the
clitoris

# Eat, Pray, Love

*Janette Hoppe*

*eat.*
the unfolding cherry
stick to the palette
a scintillating shiraz

*pray.*
he slams her head into the wall
claret dripping

        d
  o
       w
        n
her face

domestic bliss
*love.*

# Balm

*Ivy Ireland*

After the doll-body, which is after all you so why not just say so, has been ripped apart, sewn back together and stuffed with some polymer that is not quite right, somehow the mind remains to sing you back inside. And here you are, born again. A fragment — some spark — must have remained there in stasis all along. Please don't say what it is.

What brought you to this course might flood back later, no doubt at a terribly inconvenient time, yet for now: witness a terrible vacancy in the neuron firing room. You are here but you are gone. A deliberate vacancy, yet something inside grieves for the space it once held. Recovery. One day there you are, looking out the ward window thinking you will never again focus on anything remotely more expansive than the latest Nordic Noir, thinking you don't want to get your real mind back anyway as vacancy is preferable in the current political climate, when there it is: the Immensity you own. The strange largeness in sorrow. Just looming there, glancing sideways at you through the holy veils, which, after all this questing after grails, turn out to be hospital bed curtains.

The Immensity sends pokes, but the body, swilling morphine, places an embargo on anything too large for it. The body packs it all away. At the back of the linen press. And what is more real anyway — body verses mind verses spirit — is a question that should no longer be asked as it is too fraught. Also too arrogant. Arrogance has no place here. Only the body is allowed and there will be no self-reflexive anything. Ever. The Immensity persists and, even though you can't do anything about it now, what with all the strings attached to your arms gifting borrowed blood to keep your heart beating strong amongst all this weak mess, you can't simply ignore its call. And so you weep, for it seems the right thing to do in the presence of all that you can't name. Because it is the only thing you can do here in transfusion transit.

The Immensity is very patient. It waits on through all these necessary human moments, it sits and blinks through all that was and is. As beyond you as a parallel star system, as integral to you as a microscopic organelle exchange. There is nowhere the Immensity is not, so it must have been there too, when that death brought you here, your doll-body defending itself against itself at all costs. Against what now. The Immensity will wait for you to be ready once again for its magnificence. Let that be some comfort. Let that alone be your balm.

# On Duty, Off Duty

*Linda Ireland*

His is the ramrod swagger of the man
made large on the exercise of petty power.
He kids himself that the inmates
read him as one of the lads.
But the shit hits the fan
just often enough
to show them who's boss here,
where moods shift in whip crack speed.
He loves the heft of keys
jangling from the thick black belt,
notching up his victories
in the empire of the rejects.

At the end of the shift
it's an easy segue when
there's no clock on clock off
between the job and the home,
the same tense neck muscled walk
out the gate and in the door.
He wears the smell of the prison home.
He brings everything locked in
to the domestic table.
It jumps under his iron fist.
The missus knows from bitter experience
there will only ever be negotiations on his terms.

She was, has been, how many years now
frozen like a feral in the crosshairs
of his arsenal of anger,
of rage against perceived emasculations,

power denied him in all
in each of the several nothings
amounting to his unutterable life.
And she pays dearly.
The gunshot gutturals of his authority
have flayed her raw.

# Stinkwort

*Judy Johnson*


After he took what he took that night
        behind the shearing shed, her little
                container of self spilled over and
        accusation followed, will follow
                now till the end of her days.  Shame's smell
                        is barn-owl, camphor and blood-lust.  Shame's
name is 'noxious weed'.  No-one blamed him
        though it was he who opened her pouch
                of seeds, and threw them all to the wind.


Now she is both anathema and
        attractant to those men who perceive
                their scythes grow larger with each pass of
                        the blade.  Don't let anyone tell you
de-flowering happens only once.  The
        petals re-grow, yellow and brown just
                to be torn down again.  But this is
                        no story of victimisation.
                                She isn't a simpering 'Love-in-


-the-mist'.  She does persist in sickening
        the few who insist on consuming
                her down to the bone.  But any self-
                        respecting crone can poison a mob
of stupid sheep.  Anger is virile
        and holy, it's true.  But revenge is
                a more sterile companion.  Don't crush
                        her defenses, just leave her alone.
                                It is all she has ever wanted.

# Unspoken Things

*Gabrielle Journey Jones*

There are things
Mostly silenced fears
Sometimes truth
That we are afraid of being perceived:
Anxious, overwhelmed, overprotective.
We dare not admit any of this to ourselves.
Therefore, they can never be written
They can never be rehearsed or spoken
They remain consciously unknown.

There are things
Mostly heart sorrows
Sometimes truth
That we have endless words
In the shape of poems about.
Stashed in dark corners of our house
They surprise us when we forgetfully
Unearth them during annual clean outs.
But we cannot bring ourselves to read them
At least never, ever out loud.

There are things
Mostly personal trauma
Sometimes truth
That we doubt others can bear our telling.
We are continually unsure about permissions
In this society sick and swelling
Bloated with the stench of secrets
We are expected to leave unspoken.

# In the Wardrobe's Secret Darkness

*Jean Kent*

My clothes in the wardrobe's secret darkness
parable the lives I have led.
For too long skins I have not shed
have hung in the dark,
jostling like the torn, thin wings
of balsa aeroplanes, butterfly-drifting
from vanished brothers' rooms
in the breezes which lift from my dreams
on unguarded nights.

Bell-bottom trousers, sweetheart necklines,
mini-skirts and hot pants —
these I lost several housemoves ago.
Who lives long enough in one web now
to hang on it a whole life-history?

Where now a white work-moth of too-easily
wearied linen lets its floral cutwork
discreetly stroll
shoulder to shoulder,
starchily denying a desire for flight,

once flapped peasant skirts,
paisley paddocks whooping with youth.
Over them drooped sleeves
as full as angels' trumpets:
dizzy as honeyeaters draining daturas,
my hands flared out,
dripping some drug called love.

Now, clutching soft shoulders
of costumes current,
I see other dresses
still waiting to dance.
My old selves, shy as skeletons,
prop up the wall.  A chill drift,
this long-lost shift ...
At seventeen, inside its fall,
I was silent.  It was a fashion
for the time, an aqua skim
as pure as water
hiding a coral reef.
Waiting to hear the world,
my thoughts like neon-flashing fish
flicked through catacombs of childhood,
diving and bubbling, preparing to leave
for a tropic burst of air.

How now could I wear
such fit-and-flair?
Such simplicity
cut so close to the heart,
such longing swirling round me,
swelling beyond my feet
until I toggled inside it
like the tongue of a bell, too shy
to speak against its hopeful hug, too thin
to ricochet off its bold rim and ring ...

Now my clothes, ghosting their hangers
queue up the lives to which it led.
From careful copies of my mother
to the see-through slouch down streets
protesting – alone, crowded round,

in a skin as thin
as a wounded lily,
safety-pinning badges
as if like beetles they might bite,
deeply to naked truth.

Someone thumbs satin in an Op Shop,
practising poverty.
Swishing a skirt of knives,
someone pleats her dreams,
pocketing them through days
decorated with dollars.  Someone sews
an eternity of white cotton
and marries it.  Years erupt in fevers
of floral prints.  Wars and détentes
bristle from folds of velvet —
its sensitivities sleeping now,
its dark nap by experience
more subtly stroked.

Now along their splintery slide,
the hangers clack.
Fabrics, buoyed by gasps of thought,
rush for take-off
and crash.  The wardrobe's too small,
the swish of time too fast.

Every seven years should I have called
the Flick man?  Emerged from their pupal shells,
clumsily crumpled, wanly wise —
here hang decades of flights now stilled.
Sheath them in a shimmer as final
as spider's silk —
one quick wrist-flick and they should vanish.

Into the hungry mouth of a Lifeline bin,
forty years of dying drift.

Darkly my hands
fill with their patterns –
as equivocal and fleeting,
as inevitably webbed

as insects' wings.

# Mother tongue

*Catherine Knight*

My mother's language
is not the same as mine.
My daughter's language
is likewise different.
Though not so unlike
we cannot communicate
(most of the time).

There are words I will
not say where they can hear.
And I know this is
true for both of them too.
For I have listened
in secret, catching shards
of their other selves
shining bright into my ears.

Our tongues echo
across generations
as we all listen
toward understanding

# Dine with Me

*Taschka Galactika Lawlor*

Dine with me, on me, in me.
Feasting on physical affection.
Lips to tips, mouth to skin, tongue to flesh.
Skin, muscle, bone.  Bodies being consumed.

Indulging breath, sight, sound and touch,
in conscious connection with another.
As the sacred masculine and feminine;
coupling, bonding, uniting as one.

The universe of yin and yang,
making love with the rhythm of all we are.
The light, the dark, the love, the fear.
The strong, the shy, the shining, the silence.

Tasting, sipping, supping, nibbling.
To devour and be devoured.
Grazing, gulping, guzzling, gorging.
Swallowed up by the pleasure of loving connection.

The warrior's body upon the goddess,
strong yet tender, firm yet flexible.
Hands to heart, chest to breast, closely beating,
with the ebb and flow of merging tides.

Losing herself, losing himself,
melting into each other's energetic circuitry,
with the wonder of breath, sound and movement.
The integration of true tantra, present with all that is.

# Chucklebird

*Chris Mansell*

```
a chucklebird a
greengirl bounc
ing heavy bodie
d bowergirl she
knows she wants
his skinny shin
y arse that ave
nue parvenu but
                baby blue until
                another and she
                too booty two s
                he wants him to
                he desperate an
                d pretty quiver
                nerved eagertop
                lease as a brid
                            e he sings chru
                            cccckk and sexy
                            struts his neck
                            out do you do y
                            ou want to to t
                            o o they do the
                            y do those shin
                            y flanks that w
                                        hoohoo blue she
                                        the first comes
                                        down to and too
                                        she two comes t
                                        oo but oo he is
                                        the thing and s
                                        oon more greeny
                                        girls comeswoon
```

# Afternoon Ferry

*Chris Mansell*

afternoon ferry
hips a wharf go
es feral in the
light a wondero
us jam of metal
and wood old as
churns chokes a
nd stops breath

    ing diesel damn
    ed dreams spilt
    portside sharks
    blister hopeful
    as angels sharp
    eyed for fallen
    fruit oh artful
    death you are a

        sudden dancer s
        o accurate blit
        he and wily you
        hide in the sun
        shine scoop the
        skim of days be
        fore the armist
        ice of age it i

            s the quiet ter
            ritory of shame
            in being mortal
            which drives us
            to desire the s
            hark nudges the
            ferry hope jags
            exits starboard

# My Final Song

*Jenny Markwell*

*Think about a woman's life as being her music and the words she says or even
doesn't say as being her song…*

She's standing in a corner,
see her back is safe that way.
She won't engage in small talk,
she's got no words to say.
She cannot meet the eyes of friends
or folk she doesn't know.
She's always waiting for the pain
– that out of nowhere blow.

She wears a lot of makeup,
paint helps to hide his sin.
She favours stand up collars
because how does she begin
to excuse those dreadful bruises,
the one's that fit his hand.
When did her dreams of love become
this bloody, violent stand!

She'll try again tomorrow
just as she does each day.
She'll cook his favourite breakfast
and she'll laugh her pains away.
She'll offer something silly
- altercation with a door.
She knows, he knows he did it,
just like all the days before.

He tells her every morning
"This crap is all your fault.
If you could be a better wife
to glorify, exalt
and honour me as I see fit
- this household's reigning king.
Were you a better butterfly
I wouldn't have to sting!"
Her friends, she wonders at the word,
why can't they see what's wrong?
Is she the only one that hears
the violence in his song?
They only see his "happy face",
his version for the crowd.
They never see her broken, bleeding,
crying, crouching, cowed.

Sometimes she thinks just one more blow
would offer sweet relief,
when thoughts of tiny innocents
come creeping like a thief.
So far his anger's left untouched
their gorgeous baby skin.
But she's smart enough to know that there's
a monster deep within.

So I'll lie here in this corner
and I'll cry my useless tears.
Then I'll wash and set the table,
cook the dinner, fetch the beers.
I'll try and watch the things I say,
the colours that I wear.
I'll clean the house more carefully
– pretend I'm just not there.

My little ones will grow up fast
as time itself decrees
but whilst they're babes, still young enough
to learn upon my knees,
I'll try and teach them love can be
honest, gentle, true;
You do not have to scream and bleed
to prove that I love you.
The years have gone, the babes have grown
and I am long since dead.
I simply lacked the courage and
believed the lies he said.
The people that I called my friends
that chose just not to see,
I wonder how they sleep at night.
Do their dreams remember me?

His temper just got out of hand,
he hit me once too hard.
My head went through a window pane,
the end a simple shard.
The life I lived was all in vain,
the cycle echoes long.
Why can't you understand my music?
Why can't you hear my final song?

# The Longest War

*Jill McKeowen*

I've wanted to say *I'm sorry, Mum,*
for tirading you those nights
when I came home from uni
inflamed with new ideas,

accusing you at the stove
of not knowing
the oppression of cooking dinner
without question.

You sighed, lifting lids
from steaming pots while I
insisted that you listen to
my half-baked lecture.

Leave me alone, you pleaded.
All I want...
is to get these potatoes cooked!
and I saw a tear evaporate

from your cheek. (You never cried
in front of us). Too close
for comfort, full of myself,
I blamed the patriarchy.

First-in-family, I knew it all
but now I understand how
your division of labour, tied to its time
and what you knew, kept us

simply fed for better things.

# The Memorable Vacay

*Alex Morris*

Locked me out of your holiday house
Locked eyes
Took me for a drive
Pushed my shoulders into asphalt
And then refused to kiss me hard ...
even when I asked nicely
even when I begged

Pitstop,
fuel,
fuck
breakup
breakdown
Departures

Knocked my heart into my feet
Watched them drag me through security
You were shaking and smiling

Said this was important so that
I'd never forget you

I drank until they seatbelt sign went dark
Then I cried up and down the aisles
poured my pride into the Atlantic,
landed in Atlanta.

Never looked back, but
Now I lock eyes with strangers
And I see you on every street

# The Audience

*Shaylie Pryer*

So many can never find the words, the feelings
because if they speak, what they know
 It becomes a solidified highlight reel
and not just a spiel, a tale told in the confines of safety to a
person with a ticket that transforms them into the audience.

They devour the reel of desperation and despair
The hurt child deep inside that starts through the mind, and
leaks through the pours of your adult body, it paralyses you with
fear, ruins your relationships, destroys the peaceful nights
and waking moments.

It slaps you with a ghost hand and phantom pain, reaching from
the past to remind you in the present that it still lingers
they are still there, and they always will be, that it is their job to
inflict pain.

Just one moment, one semblance of safety, is when the person
with the ticket shows up to your screening, reaches for that
ghost hand, and instead of twisting and pushing it away like you
always beg, plead and scream to do
they grab the hand, hold it and say:

"This trauma is real, not a show, not a highlight reel, I will guide
your scenes, your desperate cries and pleas, and I will help your
child heal"

# Secrets

*Rhiannon Pryor*

The truth is sore arms

                   and bleeding gums,

blood red abortions.
But you don't want to hear that.
Blissfully ignorant and unaware
in your bubble-wrap world.
The truth is bad teeth

                   and stomach cramps.

That's my secret.

                   You don't want to

know.
And I don't want to tell.

# Musical Beds

*Debbie Robson*

She says goodnight and closes the door
her tiny hand barely reaching the knob
her whole body stretched tall to close
the door, to fill the dimensions of my role.
And here I am lying in her bed, in a reverse
world to my own. The door opens again
I glance up, sleep tight she adds, and I smile.

# Deconstruct

*Michele Seminara*

Hair
traitorous grey
shameful need to pretend anti ageing.

Plucking, dilapidating; dyeing, dying.

Betrayal of knees, hands, feet, neck (knees!)

circled & magnified, almost expired
   — quick sale!

The male body needing no such revision.
His landscape a shameless prairie
defining horizons, bristling grass.

# Stew

*Kerri Shying*

I am back        to listening        behind
a wall   to laughter       my boy
  friend he's known since
  they were four

back home        suddenly
holed up      talking      I hear

the way I listened for his sounds
at eight weeks   at one year

at two am    when worry was
around my heart like fat

and I was dying of the
  teenage years

we both exist alone    two pots
simmering of the same stock

have added these flavours      distinct

I lay in bed     listen
in the headiness

# Manifest

*Melinda Smith*

If you must make me,
draw me forth through that
needle's eye

have a care for this raw skin
what abrades it, how
it may be sliced and sutured

I was pure electricity, pure simian ululation
If you must cage me
box and bottle me

franken-birth me
in a clumsy bucket
you will learn the sorrow of mangle and botch

of the warp and the scorch mark.

You will see it is no sorrow.

With luck I may multiply

I may layer, matrix, palimpsest
I may go choral, become geology
Take your hand from me

set me among a swarm of eyes
As they move over me
they will mark me, too.

# I Love This Aussie Bushland

*Sherynne Smith*

I love this Aussie Bushland,
All green and gold and brown,
Being one with nature,
Never gets me down.
Lizards scurry up Gum Trees,
While birds twitter gaily overhead,
Leaves falling to the ground,
Create a deep, soft bed.
Ponds and streams and rivers,
Dot the land everywhere,
Sucking on juicy Eucalypt leaves,
You will find Koalas.
Snakes go slithering in the bush,
Quietly through the day,
We wear hefty hiking boots,
And stay out of their way.
Wide blue oceans are nearby,
Waves crashing on the shore,
Surfies paddling through the wash,
To ride them they are sure.
Back on land the sun is hot,
Beating on my skin,
I pick up litter here and there,
From someone else's sin.
I love this Aussie Bushland,
All green and gold and brown,
Being one with nature,
Never gets me down!

# Sugar Daddy

*Beth Spencer*

Come visit, you said
Would you come visit if I sent you a ticket?

Paris streets, walking in my Doc Martens
The smell of sex, the stairs, the pastry shops

Striding, with nowhere to go
(just away from you)

Easy pickings for men trying to pick me up
Really? You would say when I returned

The abuse
The apologies

Once I did see some police beating up a man
Stop it! I yelled. They looked at me

stunned that I would interfere
Then continued with what they were doing

You continued
We always continued

And in a cafe, my first cup of coffee in five years
I'll keep the sugar

after all I paid for it.

# Plenary

*Gillian Swain*

She misses insomnia
like insomniacs crave sleep.
Lives her dreams in daylight,
speaks truth
naked   void of fluff.
Strips you of inhibition
delivers you to reality
with a thud.

She knows sadness and death and cold
and the truth that darkness brings.
She knows earth and Mother and power,
and that they are the same.
She's almost surprised that you
don't.

As generous as forever
gentle as the dawn
and as strong as the promise of friendship.
She's fierce
the way she stands her ground
unwavering    unwanting    uncensored.
And as loyal as blood is red.

There are never enough minutes in a day
to complete her weavings,
thread all her webs
of magic   history   trust.
She knows   earth   Mother   power.
She misses insomnia
like insomniacs
crave peace.

# Sleeping Beauty

*Sarah Temporal*

She heard life going on
outside. The muted mutterings of
other people's lives. She couldn't
describe her own strife if she tried -
      All had stopped.
Ground down to nothing.
You see, Sleeping Beauty
did not fall peacefully

into that deep dream that took
her self and her identity.
For though we called her beautiful
her thoughts were sometimes ugly:
Guilt. Despair. Melancholy.
And sure, that's ordinary,
but it didn't fit her story so she
kept it all inside. Terrorised

by a night-time of the mind
that lasted a hundred years.
And though she gave no sign,
She was feeling
everything.

It's just that kind of spell.
Once it gets you,
you can't ask for help.

So I wonder what she wanted
just before she tempted fate:
Maybe
          just a moment
Maybe
          just a friend to ask
if she's ok —
                she wasn't.

Now all round her
castle, the gardens are choked
with lantana. It hardens and climbs
entangles with vines
strangles the sunlight
blacks out the outside
her bedroom lays darkly enchanted.

All her treasures, once-cherished,
are buried in dust. Nothing
is touched. Discarded clothes and
ambitions, pictures of herself
as a different person.

She can't make
anything
happen. Can't
wake. Can't move. Can't speak.
Her kingdom lies in ragged piles at her feet
but she thinks that it's probably her fault.
Because she just kept spinning that spinning wheel
chasing that giddy feeling
Silly girl! Playing with spindles!
Fiddling with fate!
She slipped and pricked a finger,

we were
too late.

I too
lived through
this long night of the mind.
I have seen days, months, years go by
without really opening my eyes.
So I know that Sleeping Beauty
did not fall peacefully

into that deep dream that took
her self and her identity.
I wonder what she wanted
just before she tempted fate:
Maybe
       just a moment
Maybe
       just anyone to ask
if she's ok —
            she wasn't.
She couldn't bear to be awake. But
She needs you to stay with her
before the spell can break.

# Closure

*Peta Van Drempt*

Verse 1:
Awoken by Vivaldi on a morning like any other
Barely opening my eyes I fall into a suit
The morning chorus cries out for you
And I can hardly move

Verse 2:
Habit draws me out into the kitchen that still remembers
And the microwave reflects the years written on my face
A splash of water doesn't wash them away
But it helps me face another day

Pre-chorus:
This is just a shell of all we used to have
But I know we'll never get it back

Chorus:
Where can you go when home is no longer here
What can you say when the conversation is over
I just talk to myself as I wait here for closure

Verse 3:
My suitcase decides that it can't pack itself
And I'm afraid that I'm no help
Some days I do pretty well
But today it reminds me that I am not myself

Pre-chorus:
I live in a shell of all we used to have
But I know we'll never get it back

Chorus:
Where can you go when home is no longer here
What can you say when the conversation is over
I just talk to myself as I wait here for closure

Bridge:
There's a train that takes me away
For a day I can pretend it'll all be okay
I'll return to find you there
And we'll make up for what we missed
Let all the gaps be filled
'cause I know I should've kissed you more
Now I know I never will

Chorus:
Where can you go when home is no longer here?
What can you say when the conversation is over?
I just talk to myself as I wait here for closure

# Winter

*Anne Walsh*

I was born in snow
grew up like a pine tree
small sapling under ice
it wasn't cold
it was warm
winter is empathetic
she speaks Snow
which is Artesian
for the silence that wells up.

# From the fall a poet rises up

*Cecilia White*

They said the angle of your fall
A piked twist towards midnight
Opened your skin, revealing substance
But not like a book: neat chapters and steady flow
Of words (although Fluxists would be offended
Claiming they broke invisible sounds
By dancing on agitation's rim, lifting texture
Beyond bodies of work, sometimes even
Dipping beneath boards to seed themselves
Into memory or clouds). They said
You have been the sky and are
Shifting under atmospheric pressure


Every generation knows the mill of perpetuity
Grinding space into a type of silt
To suffocate the eye, encase the heart
(Perhaps the Beat Poets were pounding
From the inside, howling a haunted distance
They're nearly all dead now, still
Close enough to shift the breath of nations
Claiming room for others (are you sure?)
Like yourself, writing in ungainly breaks
From trips in the dark that fracture expression
To lift an earthly force above the place
You landed in that uncontrolled movement
Between yourself and every urgent else

Was it excitement or perhaps fear
That wrote emotion into your veins
Formed new bones in your work
Pressed a voice into your emerging scars
Enough to make Gutenberg want to return
For the next revolution. And your uprising.

# Open the window and let her fly out

*Georgina Woods*

Falena you're beating your wings on my ear for escape.
Your hunters are taken in custody. Go now, you
friable moon slave: stop bumping your head on the glass.
Your liberty shivers in silvery gloom with my own and
my young friend whose dad told me, Men are just visual
in his relief that she's pretty enough to attract one.
I'm watching them watching themselves being watched as
                                        they preen.
Shivering wing-hems and brushing their downy soft
thigh hairs for comfort, or fiddling the clasp of a bracelet.
Falena, the silvery ball that they gave you is not the moon.
Put it away from you. It would enthral you with
mirror-light caught from your ersatz self: shiny and eye-
                                        catching.
Its surface is polished with touching but passionless.
Nestled in moth suede it's poised to be grabbed and
put on display with a pin through the abdomen.

# Endangered Species

*Janette Hoppe*

I am part of a dying breed
an endangered species known as woman

I am a #metoo story too many
that makes ignorance bliss
making sure that we switch the blame
to the victim and from the perpetrator
because you know these feminine campaigns
are created by man haters
yes, I am part of a dying breed

I am part of a dying breed
an endangered species known as woman

55 women have died in Australia so far this year
and I am just a heartbeat away
from being another statistic
and it's hard to remain optimistic
when there is more moral outrage over a plastic bag
than this life that I've been gifted
yes, I am part of a dying breed

I am part of a dying breed
an endangered species known as woman

But it's time to flip the switch on this script
and take women off the endangered list
let's ensure that our women are protected
What arm do I have to give to ensure that our women are
                                              respected?
It's time to eradicate this violence
and make a stance
after all —
                    'It's because of her we can!'

*55 is the total of all women killed by violence so far this year in Australia
(18 December 2019: Destroy the Joint — Counting Dead Women).

# Biographical notes

DAEL ALLISON writes poetry, fiction and essays and is completing a PhD on the Literature of the Hunter region. Back in the 70s the feminist resurgence brought feist, hope and determination to achieve equality and an end to domestic violence within three generations. We have to keep fighting.

MAGDALENA BALL is a novelist, poet, reviewer and interviewer. She is the Managing Editor of *Compulsive Reader*. She has been widely published in literary journal, anthologies and online; and is the author of several published books of poetry and fiction including most recently *High Wire Step* (Flying Island Press, 2018) and *Unreliable Narratives* (Girls on Key Press, 2019).

LISA BARRON grew up in Redhead with a passion for writing. Lisa's harsh and unusual life inspires her poetry and takes readers to unexpected places, to the thin surface of mind and reality. Lisa has poems and short stories published online in *The Light of Love*. Her debut book *The Tatter of Life* is a story of universal truth and was published in 2018. Lisa's poems featured in the original *Women of Words – Eat, Stray'd, Love* chapbook 2016.

L.E. BERRY (LOUISE BERRY) has had her poetry published in various anthologies including *Women of Words*, *Women's Work*, *Margaret Olley poems*, *Eucalypt*, *Food for Thought*, *Grevillea & Wonga Vine*, *Australian Poetry Collaboration*, *A Slow Combusting Hymn*, *To End all Wars*, *Australian Poetry Collaboration*, and various community anthologies. Her first poetry collection, *Channelling Childhood* has recently been published by Ginninderra Press.

KELLY BLANEY-MURPHY: Having dispensation to borrow books from the adult section at the local public library and deliberately getting lost on horseback, so that she could loose the reins and let the horse find his own way home, are two of Kelly's favourite memories from her Western Australian childhood. Kelly now works as a writer on NSW's Central Coast, where she creates puzzles as well as articles for Lovatts Media and is learning orienteering.

LISA CALLISTER claims that she is the world's worst pencil and paint artist, an incurable overthinker with a life-long inability to understand society's thought processes. Considered by others to be caring, fun, loyal, compassionate, vivacious and strong minded; she knows who she is and is resilient and insightful. Considered by her Nan as "always just a bit different to the others". Considered by her dog to be impatient and forthcoming with steamed veges. She considers herself as someone who is still trying to find where she fits and should really have a good nap.

Jan Dean lives in a suburb in Lake Macquarie. She was the first female president and is a life member of Poetry at the Pub Newcastle. Widely published, her writing appears in *Meanjin, Southerly, Rabbit Poetry* and Newcastle Poetry Prize anthologies.

GLORIA DEMILLO is a poet and spoken word artist. They've worked with Red Room Poetry, Word Travels, Bankstown Poetry Slam, and founded UNSW Poetry Slam. Gloria's most notable contributions include the Harana Poetry Tour for the Art Gallery of New South Wales; published works in *Cordite Poetry Review*; *UNSWeetened 2014*; Bankstown Poetry Slam's anthologies *On Second Thought* and *The Resurrection*; and performances at Sydney International Women's Poetry and Arts Festival, Wollongong Writers Festival, Glebe Street Fair, and the Bankstown Poetry Slam Olympics.

MEG DUNN's poetry thematics are all over the shop – political, dream-scapes, personal frissons – and are mostly too long to fit into magazine submissions. She makes her own stylistic rules but is conscious of the supreme importance of good craft. She's been at it for quite some time, from co-founding Newcastle's Poetry at the Pub back in the '80's, to enjoying many years in the halcyon days of the Melbourne scene, where she won best Spoken Word at the Melbourne Fringe and helped organise the legendary Overload Festival. She currently resides in Tamworth in rural NSW and has not written any bush poetry. She is completing her long-form poetry manuscript *Basic Aeronautical Knowledge* with the help of her flying instructor.

ANNA FORSYTH is an editor, writer and poet originally from Auckland. She is a founder of feminist poetry organisation, Girls on Key and her latest poetry collection is *Beatific Toast* (Girls on Key Press, 2018).

DEBRA HELY: When the chaos in life subsides, Debra returns to writing. It's her major creative outlet, even when used in her work. Any genre considered. Sometimes she ends up with a finished product that even she is proud of.

JANETTE HOPPE is the creative director of Papatuanuku Press. Papatuanuku Press is a creative platform that oversees many projects such as: The Poetry Bomb, The Blue Series Projects and Women of Words. Each of these unique projects aim in creating healing spaces through creativity.

IVY IRELAND is the author of *Incidental Complications and Porch Light*. Ivy's awards include the Australian Young Poet Fellowship, the Harriet Jones Memorial Prize, the Thunderbolt Prize and she was runner-up in the 2019 UC International Poetry Prize. Ivy completed her Ph.D. in 2012 and her poetry, essays and reviews float about the internet and various literary journals and anthologies.

LINDA IRELAND is a member of Lake Macquarie's Blue Room Poets. She helped establish Poetry at the Lake Mac Pub, now in its 5th year. Her work has appeared in several anthologies.

JUDY JOHNSON has published eight poetry collections and a novel. Her book prizes include the Victorian Premier's award, shortlisting in the WA and NSW Premier's awards and the Wesley Michel Wright prize (twice). Her verse novel *Jack* was on the syllabus of Sydney and Melbourne University and her latest book *Dark Convicts* explores the life and times of her two African American First Fleet Ancestors.

GABRIELLE JOURNEY JONES is a spoken word poet, percussionist and event producer born on sovereign Gadigal Land, Sydney, Australia. She is from Maori and African American bloodlines and lives in the Far South Coast, NSW. Gabrielle is wholeheartedly inspired by and contributes to diverse creative communities which celebrate inclusion, activism and compassion.

JEAN KENT grew up in rural Queensland and now lives at Lake Macquarie, NSW. Eight books of her poetry have been published: the most recent is *Paris in my Pocket* (PSP 2016).

CATHERINE KNIGHT is a member of Poetry at the Pub and has been known to read poetry at those events. Her work is published in some of the PatP anthologies.

TASCHKA GALACTIKA LAWLOR is an emerging artist. She has been writing since she was young and found spoken word a few years ago to give her poetry a voice, her voice. She has read at Word in Hand, weddings, funerals and various other events and gatherings. Amongst her work in community service administration, massage and coaching, she is a spiritual seeker and philosophical free spirit who loves to ponder and explore many areas of life's journey; such as the human condition, the healing arts, neuroscience, nature, magic, music, mantras, yoga and dance.

CHRIS MANSELL's new book *101 Quads* will appear with Puncher & Wattmann/Thorny Devil Press in 2020.

JENNY MARKWELL is a writer and performance poet of Bush Poetry. Her main interests are in subjects pertaining to women and mothers – how they feel and act – and in the field of women surviving domestic violence and its associated mental health issues.

JILL McKEOWEN is a Newcastle poet. Her poems are in several anthologies, including *Grieve, Poetry & Place, The Olley Poems,*

*To End All Wars*, and several Newcastle Poetry at the Pub anthologies. She works full-time at the University of Newcastle, where she teaches academic writing.

ALEX MORRIS is a leather-wearing vegetarian who thrives on red wine, black coffee and spontaneity. She likes reading poems written by people she knows.

SHAYLIE PRYER is a 23 year old social justice advocate working at Community Disability Alliance Hunter and studies social work. She is passionate about areas of disability and inclusion rights, mental health and trauma. She tries to convey these themes through individual perspective and personal experiences.

RHIANNON PRYOR: Born 1979 in rural Australia she has been described as a Brutal Novocastrian Beat Poet and called every other name under the sun. Sometimes she paints, sometimes she writes, occasionally she does something with it.

DEBBIE ROBSON has been writing poems since the 1990's. She has performed some of her poems on radio, at Sydney Poetry events, in the Blue Mountains and more recently as part of the Women of Words project in Newcastle.

MICHELE SEMINARA is a poet and Managing Editor of online creative arts journal *Verity La*. She has published a full-length collection, *Engraft* (Island Press, 2016) and two chapbooks: *Scar to Scar* (written in collaboration with Robbie Coburn, Press Press, 2016) and *HUSH* (Blank Rune Press, 2017). Her second full-length collection, *Suburban Fantasy* is forthcoming from UWA Publishing in October 2020.

KERRI SHYING is a Newcastle-based writer of Chinese/Wiradjuri/Australian family. Her books are *Sing Out When You Want Me*, 2017 (Flying Island Press/Cerberus/ASM), *Elevensies*, 2018 (Puncher and Wattman) and *Knitting Mangrove Roots*, 2019 (Flying Island/Cerberus/ASM).

MELINDA SMITH has published seven books of poetry, most recently *Goodbye, Cruel* (Pitt Street Poetry, 2017) and *Listen, bitch* (Recent Work Press, 2019). Her work has been widely anthologised and translated; her selected poems in Chinese, *Perfectly Bruised* (完美瘢痕) is launching at NWF 2020. She is based in the ACT and is a former poetry editor of *The Canberra Times*. She won the 2014 Prime Minister's Literary Award for poetry.

SHERYNNE SMITH is a mother, grandmother, writer, aromatherapist and healer with a burning desire for writing. She is a lover of people of all ages, animals from dogs to snakes and all things natural. You will often find Sherynne toiling away in her Community 'Garden of Healing', caring for family, neighbours and friends or volunteering for a local cause. Sherynne enjoys the vast beauty of Earth, the sea and walking contemplatively through a forest.

BETH SPENCER's books include *Vagabondage* (UWAP), *How to Conceive of a Girl* (Random House) and most recently, *Never Too Late* (PressPress). She writes fiction, poetry essays and writing for radio and performance. She has won a number of awards, including the Carmel Bird Digital Literary Award in 2018 for her short fiction collection *The Age of Fibs*, now a Spineless Wonders ebook. She lives in the Central Coast NSW. www.bethspencer.com. *Sugar Daddy* was first published in *Pink Cover Zine* and in Beth's chapbook *Never Too Late* (PressPress, 2018).

GILLIAN SWAIN spent much of her childhood daydreaming and playing along the shores of Lake Macquarie between Warners Bay and Speers Point. She now lives with her husband and four children in the Maitland area, where they run a successful coffee roastery and Gillian is the poet in residence at a local café. Gillian's work appears in various anthologies, shared first place in the Maclean's booksellers award in the HWC 2019 Grieve project and has a chapbook *Sang Up* by Picaro Press. Her first longer collection was the recently published pocket-book *My skin its own sky* by Flying Island Press.

SARAH TEMPORAL is a performance poet and poetry educator from Murwillumbah NSW. She is the winner of the 2018 Nimbin Performance Poetry World Cup and the author of *SlamCraft*. Sarah initiated and runs Poets Out Loud, an event and project platform for writers in the Tweed region.

PETA VAN DREMPT is a singer-songwriter, piano accompanist and founder of Peta's Piano (petaspiano.com), a library of piano backing tracks for students. Through her songs she relishes the challenges of shining a light on the beauty in life's ordinariness. She is also deeply passionate about helping others own their creative journey, particularly through her mentoring work with the students she accompanies.

ANNE WALSH has been shortlisted twice for the ACU Prize in Literature and for The Newcastle Poetry Prize. Her work has appeared in *Cordite, Mascara, The Canberra Times, Backstory, Other Terrain, Verity La, Poem & Dish, FemAsia, Not Very Quiet, Pink Cover Zine, Heroines Anthology* (Neo Perennial Press), *Monologue Adventure, Glimmer Train* (U.S.). Books: *I Love Like a Drunk Does* (Ginninderra Press, '09), *Intact* (Flying Island Books, '17).

CECILIA WHITE is an Australian poet and artist.

GEORGINA WOODS is an environmentalist and poet living and working on Worimi and Awabakal land, in Newcastle. She has a PhD in English Literature from Newcastle University and works in environmental advocacy with people and communities affected by coal and gas mining.